Women
OF THE BIBLE

Written by Lorinda James, BMid, MCouns, MSwSt
Photography & Graphic Design by Jess Meek, BFA(Film and Television)
Biblical Content Consulting and Editing by Rev. Allan Quak, BDiv, MA(Th)
Copy Editing by Kierstin Ham, BSpPath(Hon)
Props & Costumes by Julie Wilson, BA

A PROJECT OF
NORTHSIDE EVANGELICAL CHURCH

Women
OF THE BIBLE

When we started this project, we had no idea that it would end up here. We are not authors, designers or professional photographers. We are just a group of four friends who lead the 'Sisterhood' Youth Girls ministry in our church. In our yearly planning meeting, back in 2016, we started talking about the incredible women of the Bible and how often their stories were overlooked. This discussion sparked an idea— a photoshoot where we would sit with our girls, read a biblical woman's story and portray them in a photograph.

The success of the Sisterhood event lead to the same activity at a women's retreat, then a third, and a fourth church event. By this time, we started to realise that these photos could evolve into a project that would reach more than just our immediate church community. After a few hundred hours researching and writing, designing, capturing and editing photos, and prayer, this book has been a labour of love that we are so excited to be able to share.

Our prayer is that by reading these women's stories you can see God's work and be encouraged in your walk with God.

Table of Contents

How to use this book:

This book has been designed to be studied as either an individual, or as a small group. On each page you will find a photographic portrayal of the woman, an overview of her story, and a reference to where the woman is mentioned in the Bible.

The questions below have been developed to help guide your reflections and discussions as you read each of these women's stories. There are many different ways to study the Bible, for this book we have chosen four main areas of focus: Context, Character & Qualities, Purpose, and Application.

The more you examine the context around the lives these women lived, their character, and their qualities, the more incredible each of them become. While none of these women were perfect, their stories highlight the character of God and show the depth and development of their faith.

Context

1. What time period or law governed God's people when this woman lived? Was there a Godly leader?

2. What were the culture and practices of the people at this time? Who did the people worship?

3. What was the role of women in this time? What were the expectations of how they lived or what they did?

Character & Qualities

1. What do we know about this woman in terms of her relationship with God, family members, and the community?

2. When faced with difficulties, how does this woman respond? Does the woman display Christ-like qualities? What would have been the response of the people at the time to her actions?

3. How does this woman's story show her growth as a person and the development of her faith and relationship with God?

Purpose

1. What makes the woman's actions unique or worthy of recording in the history of God's people?

2. What was the wider impact of this woman's actions? How far did the results of her actions reach?

3. What does this story teach us about the character of God?

Application

1. When thinking about this woman and her life, can you identify with her? Why or why not? How are you alike, or different, from her?

2. What lessons can be learnt from this woman's relationship with God?

3. How would you respond if you found yourself in this situation instead? What would your journey with God be like?

Abigail

... may you be blessed for your good judgement.

Abigail was an Israelite woman who was born around 1040BC. Married to Nabal, a cruel and unwise man, Abigail is distinguished by her beauty and intelligence.

During the struggle between David and Saul for the throne of Israel Samuel the prophet died. As David travelled to attend Samuel's burial he and his men came to Nabal the Calebite, of the tribe of Judah, and asked for shelter and food. David and his men had previously protected Nabal's shepherds and flocks of sheep and it was expected that Nabal would repay David for his kindness with hospitality. Instead Nabal foolishly denied them and insulted David. David responded by arming his men, preparing to attack with the intention of killing every male of Nabal's household in retribution.

Abigail was the wife of Nabal and in contrast to her husband she was wise and thoughtful. When she heard of her husband's actions, she prepared a large amount of food and wine and quickly rode out to meet David and his men. When she found David she bowed before him, begged him to forgive the actions of Nabal, and halt his attack. David listened to her and honoured her request. He blessed her and acknowledged that her wisdom and actions were godly and they had kept him from committing sin in anger.

Abigail returned home and found Nabal throwing a huge feast. He was drunk so she told him nothing of how she had saved him and their household. The next morning after Nabal had sobered Abigail revealed the consequences of his insults and told him of her actions. In that moment Nabal's heart failed and ten days later he died. David heard of this and praised God. He then sent word to Abigail and asked her to marry him. She accepted and became David's second wife.

Read Abigail's story in 1 Samuel 25:1-42.

Anna

... she worshipped day and night.

Anna was a Jewish prophetess who was born in Jerusalem around 80BC. Widowed early in her life she dedicated herself to prayer and praise.

Anna's life was one of great sorrow. Born into the tribe of Asher she married her husband at a young age. Anna was unable to bare children of her own. After seven years her husband died and Anna was left a childless widow. In her grief she turned to the Lord and instead of remarrying she decided to dedicate her life to praising Him. Anna stayed at the temple day and night to pray and fast, worshipping God unceasingly. She became known as a woman of intense faith and as a prophetess. As years turned to decades Anna remained at the temple praying for the salvation of her people, and for the Messiah who was promised to them.

When Anna was eighty-four, Mary and Joseph arrived at the temple to consecrate the infant Jesus and offer a sacrifice to the Lord. With aged eyes Anna saw the infant and immediately knew He was the promised Messiah. She recognised Him as the Son of God and came up to his parents, perhaps hoping to cradle the infant Jesus. In this moment she prophesied over Him and proclaimed to all who were in the temple that this infant was the redemption of Jerusalem. Jesus was the long awaited Saviour who would restore the kingdom and bring glory to the Lord. Anna's praise overflowed and her heart was filled with joy.

Alongside Simeon, a holy and righteous man, Anna was one of the first people to herald Jesus as the Messiah. Her long life of faithful waiting had been rewarded as she had seen the face of Jesus Christ.

Read Anna's story in Luke 2:22-39.

NEW
TESTAMENT
GOSPELS

Bathsheba

... the Lord has delivered me out of every trouble.

Bathsheba was an Israelite woman who was born around 1030BC. Portrayed as beautiful and graceful, she exuded a quiet dignity throughout the numerous trials she endured.

Twenty years after David was appointed king over all Israel, he sent his General Joab to wage war upon the Ammonites. Early one evening David saw a beautiful woman bathing upon a rooftop. The woman, Bathsheba, was the wife of Uriah the Hittite, one of David's chief warriors. David was besotted by her and summoned her to the palace. Obligated to obey the wishes of the king, Bathsheba went to the palace and he slept with her.

Soon after her night with David, Bathsheba realised she was pregnant and sent word to him. In response David summoned Uriah back from the war to give him the opportunity to lay with Bathsheba hoping that, in doing so Uriah would claim the forthcoming child as his own. However, Uriah was a man of honour and refused the embrace of his wife saying that the soldiers on the battlefield knew no such comfort and so he would not either. David sent Uriah back to the war and secretly arranged for him to be placed on the frontline. As a result Uriah was killed.

After the death of her husband Bathsheba mourned. David then summoned her once more to the palace and married her. God was enraged at David for his wickedness and as punishment for his sins the child Bathsheba carried died soon after birth. After David confessed his sins, God extended His forgiveness to him. Bathsheba remained as one of David's wives and eventually became the mother to Solomon, who later became a wise and powerful king.

Read Bathsheba's story in 2 Samuel 11:1-12:25 and 1 Kings 1:11-31.

OLD
TESTAMENT
KINGDOM

Deborah

... may all who love You Lord be like the sun.

Deborah was an Israelite woman who lived sometime around 1270BC. As a prophetess and the only female Judge, Deborah was a remarkable and unique woman.

Deborah was born into the Israelite nation during a time when it had no king. Instead judges were selected by God to provide guidance to the people. Early in her life Deborah was distinguished as a prophetess and woman of abundant faith. She became a judge and with great wisdom and courage she led her people.

One day Deborah received a word from God that a man named Barak, of the tribe of Naphtali, was to lead the armies of Israel against Jabin king of Canaan. The Canaanites, who had oppressed the Israelites cruelly for twenty years, were led into battle by General Sisera. When she summoned Barak and told him of God's plans for him, Barak was fearful. Barak declared that he would not attack the Canaanites unless Deborah was by his side. She agreed to lead the army with him but warned him that, because of his cowardice, Israel would be delivered by the hands of a woman and Barak would not gain any glory. Barak agreed to this and together they lead an army of ten thousand soldiers and won a great victory against the Canaanites. General Sisera fled in fear when his men were defeated, seeking refuge with Heber the Kenite who was an old friend. In turn Sisera was killed by Heber's wife, and with his death, the oppression of the Israelites ended. Elated and victorious Deborah praised the Lord and sang a song of exaltation. After the war Deborah continued as a judge for a further forty years and there was peace in the land of Israel. Deborah's courage and wisdom made her beloved by the nation, but it was her faith in the Lord that made her great leader.

Read Deborah's story in Judges 4:1-5:31.

OLD
TESTAMENT
KINGDOM

Elizabeth

... she exclaimed 'for nothing is impossible with God'.

Elizabeth was a Jewish woman of the Levite tribe who was born around 50BC. She was a woman of extraordinary faith, described as blameless and upright in the sight of the Lord.

In the earliest days of the New Testament a woman named Elizabeth lived with her husband Zechariah in Hebron, the hill country of Judah. They both grieved that they had not been blessed with any children. One day while Zechariah was serving at the temple the angel Gabriel came to him. Gabriel prophesied that despite their advancing age, Elizabeth would bear a son who would be filled with the Holy Spirit. Zechariah doubted the word of the angel so Gabriel removed his ability to speak. Soon after Gabriel's visit, Elizabeth became pregnant. She was overjoyed and secluded herself for five months, ceaselessly praising the Lord for His abundant blessings.

Towards the end of her pregnancy Elizabeth welcomed her relative, Mary, into her home after Mary had her own visit from the angel Gabriel. Elizabeth's faith was so great that upon greeting Mary, Elizabeth was filled with the Holy Spirit and recognised Mary as the mother of Jesus Christ. The child within Elizabeth leapt for joy as she poured blessings upon Mary.

Soon after Mary returned home, Elizabeth gave birth to her son. He was brought to the temple to be circumcised in the presence of his father Zechariah, who was still mute. Zechariah's speech was restored upon naming the baby John. This was in accordance with the instructions of the angel Gabriel. Elizabeth praised God for she knew that the Lord's hand was with her little boy who would one day grow up to be John the Baptist.

Read Elizabeth's story in Luke 1:5-25, 39-45, 57-80.

NEW
TESTAMENT
GOSPELS

Esther

… you were brought here for such a time as this.

Esther was a Judean woman who was born around 495BC. Known for both her beauty and her wisdom she faced incredible danger with dignity.

The Israelite people had hardened their hearts towards God and so He allowed them to be defeated by the Babylonians and taken into exile. For seventy years the people remained in Babylon until the Babylonians were conquered by the Persian Empire. It was then that the Judeans were permitted to travel home, though many decided to stay in the Persia. During this time a young Judean girl named Hadassah, who was more commonly known as Esther, was orphaned. Esther went to live with her cousin Mordecai, who raised her as his own daughter.

At this time King Xerxes of Persia banished his wife Queen Vashti after she disobeyed him. Eager to replace his queen, Xerxes sent officials to gather the most beautiful women they could find. As a woman of remarkable beauty Esther was found by them and sent to the palace. There she was pampered and then sent before Xerxes alongside many other young women from which Xerxes would select a new queen. Xerxes was immediately enchanted by Esther's beauty and chose her. During Esther's reign a plot was uncovered by Mordecai that would lead to the death of all the Jews in Persia. Urged by Mordecai, Esther risked death to approach Xerxes uninvited and beg for the lives of her people. Xerxes was moved by her courage and issued an edict allowing the Jews to protect themselves. In the dangerous times that followed, the Jews who remained in Persia triumphed over their enemies and grew to be a powerful force. Esther's courage as a queen, and faithfulness as God's servant, enabled her to face death to protect her people.

Read the story of Queen Esther in the book of Esther.

OLD
TESTAMENT

KINGDOM

Eunice

... I am reminded of your sincere faith.

Eunice was a Jewish woman who lived in the Galatian town of Lystra around 50AD. Her story is one of godly motherhood and faith lived by example.

Eunice's life is known only by a handful of verses in the New Testament, many of which do not even mention her by name. Eunice was born to a Jewish mother named Lois. Lois raised her daughter to be faithful and eventually arranged her marriage to an unnamed Greek man. Together they had a single child, a boy she named Timothy.

A few years later the apostle Paul was travelling through Lystra preaching and teaching about Jesus Christ. Eunice listened with great enthusiasm to these sermons and converted to Christianity along with her mother Lois. After this Eunice dedicated herself to living a life of service to God and teaching her young son the scriptures. The godly example of Christian faith Eunice demonstrated was so powerful that Timothy was converted at a young age and he grew to be a man of belief and great spiritual leadership.

When Paul returned to Lystra a few years later Eunice's son Timothy went with him and under Paul's mentorship, became a renowned evangelist. Throughout his writings to Timothy, Paul credits Timothy's childhood in a home that honoured the Lord and read the Scriptures. This was the foundation of Timothy's salvation and the groundwork for the mighty deeds he was able to accomplish in the name of Jesus Christ. Eunice's life is an important reminder of the gentle influence of a godly mother upon her children, and the dedication it takes to raise children who know and fear the Lord.

Read Eunice's story in Acts 16:1-3, 2 Timothy 1:5 and 2 Timothy 3:14-15.

OLD
TESTAMENT

CHURCH

Eve

... and she shall be called woman.

Eve was the first woman on earth. Created by God Himself in utter perfection, she is the mother of all humanity.

On the sixth day of creation the Lord God created Adam, the first man, from dust. Distinguished from all the other creatures on earth Adam had no companion. God decided that it was not good for Adam to be alone and God's final act of creation was to form Eve. After placing Adam into a deep sleep, God removed one of his ribs and from this He created Eve. Eve was never a child but was placed upon the earth as a complete and perfect woman. Adam was delighted with his companion and together they lived in the paradise of the Garden of Eden, walking and talking with God in the cool of the evenings.

Just as Eve was the first woman upon earth, she was also the first woman to fall into the trap of temptation. Satan disguised himself as a serpent and spoke lies to Eve about her purpose and the very nature of God. Deceived by the lies of Satan, Eve began to doubt God's sovereignty. Desiring to be like God, Eve reached out and took fruit from the Tree of the Knowledge of Good and Evil and ate it. She also shared it with Adam who was with her. Together they fell from their perfection into sin. The consequence for both Adam and Eve was banishment from the Garden of Eden, and Eve was cursed by God Himself to bare children with great pains.

Although Eve committed the original sin, she still lived a long, healthy, and abundant life. She was mother to dozens of children who would go on to populate the whole earth. Her name and story are remembered forever.

Read Eve's story in Genesis 2:4-3:25.

OLD
TESTAMENT

CREATION

Gomer

... I will show my love to the one I called.

Gomer was a Jewish woman who lived around 730BC. She was a fallen woman, described as a sinner, who was redeemed by the love of her husband and by the grace of God.

During the time when Israel was split into two kingdoms, the northern kingdom prospered greatly. With wealth and power came idolatry and the people had turned their hearts away from the Lord. The prophet Hosea was the prophet to Israel. God came to him and instructed him to marry a prostitute who was to be the representation of Israel's faithlessness. Hosea obeyed and married a woman named Gomer.

After Hosea brought Gomer into his home, she bore him a son who the Lord named Jezreel, meaning 'God sows', as a reminder of the Israelite king who had rejected God. Gomer became unhappy in Hosea's household and her eyes began to wander, settling upon other men. She then gave birth to a daughter who was named Lo-Ruhamah, meaning 'unloved', and a second son Lo-Ammi, meaning 'not of my people'. With these names, not only did God demonstrate His displeasure with the Israelite people, He added to Hosea's growing suspicion that he was not the father of these children. Not long after the birth of her second son Gomer abandoned her family and returned to prostitution. Hosea remained behind and dutifully raised the children of Gomer.

Later the Lord instructed Hosea to find Gomer, who had sold herself into slavery. Hosea paid for her freedom, then brought her back into his home and lovingly restored her as his wife. Gomer was deeply moved by the actions of Hosea and repented of her sins. She was reconciled to him and stayed with Hosea as a faithful wife and loving mother for the rest of her life.

Read Gomer's story in Hosea 1:1-3:5.

OLD
TESTAMENT

KINGDOM

Hagar

... You are the God who sees me.

Hagar was an Egyptian woman who lived around 1850BC. She was a fierce mother and a woman of great faith who was willing to walk the difficult path God set before her.

God came to Abraham and made a covenant with him, promising that his descendants would be God's chosen nation. Abraham believed in the Lord but he and his wife Sarah were childless and beyond their childbearing years. Sarah lost faith that God could ever create a nation through her. Sarah had an Egyptian slave named Hagar that Abraham had purchased for her. Sarah presented Hagar to Abraham as a concubine in the hope that she could conceive a child. Hagar became pregnant and began to resent Sarah who, in turn, was jealous of Hagar and mistreated her. Unable to bear Sarah's abuse, Hagar fled into the desert and cried out to the Lord. God listened to her fears and spoke to her telling her to have faith and patience. He instructed her to return to her mistress which she did. Soon after Hagar gave birth to a son whom Abraham named Ishmael, meaning 'God listens'.

Years later, after Sarah gave birth to Isaac, she began to hate Hagar and Ishmael. Sarah told Abraham to banish them from the family. Torn between his love for his son Ishmael and the demands of Sarah, Abraham regretfully sent Hagar and her young son into the wilderness with a single bag of water and food. The water soon ran dry and, dying of thirst, Hagar placed her son under the shade of a bush and walked away, not wishing to see him perish. Hagar again cried out to the Lord who answered her prayers and provided a well for her and Ishmael to drink from. From then Hagar lived in the wilderness fiercely protecting her son until he grew into a great warrior.

Read Hagar's story in Genesis 16:1-16 and Genesis 21:8-21.

Hannah

... look upon me Lord and remember me.

Hannah was a Hebrew woman who lived in Jerusalem around 1150BC. Her life was marred by sorrow but it is her joyful and selfless sacrifice by which she is known.

There was an Israelite man of the tribe of Ephraim named Elkanah who had two wives; Hannah whom he favoured, and Penniah. Penniah had given many children to Elkanah but Hannah was barren. Hannah greatly grieved her inability to have a child and she endured much provocation from Penniah who mercilessly insulted her. Though Elkanah continually reassured Hannah of his love and favour she spent years mourning for the child she wanted.

One night Hannah went to the temple alone. She sat and prayed, begging God to bless her with a child. She vowed that if He did so she would dedicate that child to God. Her prayers were so passionate and sad that the High Priest Eli thought she was drunk and tried to send her away. When Hannah revealed the source of her grief Eli blessed her in the name of the Lord.

In the time that followed Hannah discovered she was pregnant. She gave birth to a son and named him Samuel. Her joy overflowed and Hannah never forgot God's abundant blessing in answering her prayer, nor her vow to return the child to God. So, when Samuel was weaned, she took him to the temple where he was dedicated to the Lord. Hannah returned home but Samuel remained at the temple and was raised by Eli to be a holy and righteous man. Samuel went on to become the next High Priest, a revered prophet, and the man who anointed King David. Hannah was blessed by God with other children and because of her selfless gratitude, she is known as a woman of grace.

Read Hannah's story in 1 Samuel 1:1-2:10.

Huldah

… your heart was responsive and you humbled yourself.

Huldah was a Jewish woman who was born around 660BC. She was a divine prophetess whose heart was filled with passion for the Lord God.

For generation after generation kings did great evil while they ruled over the Israelites. After the death of the detestable King Amon, his young son Josiah succeeded him. Josiah was only eight years old when he ascended to the throne. Under the guidance of his godly mother Josiah sought to do what was right in the eyes of God. During Josiah's reign scrolls containing the Book of the Law were rediscovered. It had been so long since the people had followed the Lord that they doubted if the scrolls were truly the Word of God. Josiah sent his chief advisor Hilkiah to the prophetess Huldah to seek wisdom from the Lord regarding the authenticity of the book.

Huldah was one of the last remaining faithful Jews. She was well respected among her people and ministered to them. When Hilkiah came to Huldah for wisdom she heard from God and confirmed that the scrolls were indeed His Word. Huldah prophesied of God's anger, ready to be poured out upon His faithless people. This impending wrath persuaded Josiah to do all he could to turn the hearts of the people back to the Lord. Josiah scoured the land destroying every altar and temple dedicated to idol worship. Josiah's conviction was so powerful that he became known as a man whose heart was fully turned to the Lord.

Huldah's wisdom and warning drew Josiah to repentance and forestalled her prophesy until after Josiah's reign when the people were defeated by the Egyptians. Huldah's story speaks of the importance of honesty and truth when following the will of the Lord.

Read Huldah's story in 2 Kings 22:1-23:37.

NEW
TESTAMENT
GOSPELS

Jael

... most blessed of women.

Jael was a Bedouin woman who lived among the Hebrew people around 1220BC. She was fierce and courageous, willing to act to protect God's people when the men of her generation were seized by fear.

The Hebrew people had once again done evil in the eyes of the Lord and God allowed them to be oppressed by the Canaanites, led by King Jabin and his General, Sisera. Weary from the oppression and cruelty of the Canaanites the Hebrews cried out to the Lord. God provided salvation through the wisdom and guidance of the judge Deborah along with Barak, the leader of the armies of Israel. Victory and freedom were prophesied by Deborah and in response the Hebrew army gathered and marched to war. The Canaanites were defeated and Sisera fled in fear for his life.

Living among the Hebrews was a Bedouin clan called the Kenites, led by a man named Heber, and his wife Jael. This tribe were a neutral party between the Israelites and Canaanites. Sisera sought refuge with them, believing they would protect him from the Hebrew army which pursued him. Heber was not in the camp at the time of Sisera's arrival so Jael welcomed the fearful general into her tent. Taking advantage of Jael's hospitality Sisera demanded she protect him and lie about his whereabouts. Jael agreed to his demands and graciously fed him rich food and milk. She covered Sisera with a rug and he fell into a deep sleep. As he slept Jael took a tent peg and hammer, and drove the peg through Sisera's head and into the ground.

Her brave act helped to complete the defeat of the Canaanites. Jael was honoured and praised by the Hebrews who credited her for releasing them from their oppression.

Read Jael's story in Judges 4:1-24 and Judges 5:24-27.

OLD
TESTAMENT
KINGDOM

Jairus' Daughter

... do not be afraid, just believe.

The daughter of Jairus is never referred to by name but her story has a profound impact, displaying the miraculous power of Jesus.

Jairus was a synagogue leader in Galilee during the time Jesus was conducting His ministry. Jairus knew of the great miracles Jesus had been performing all over Judea, but as a part of the synagogue leadership he had been actively involved in opposing Jesus and His ministry. Jairus had only one daughter who was about twelve years old. He loved her deeply and was distressed when she fell gravely ill. Healers could not do anything for his precious daughter and it became clear that she was near death. Jairus was faced with a difficult choice, he could let his daughter perish or plead for help from Jesus.

Desperate and afraid for his daughter Jairus found Jesus preaching to a crowd. He fell at Jesus' feet with humility and begged for Jesus to heal his daughter. Jesus agreed to help Jairus and together they made their way to the home of Jairus, eagerly followed by the crowd. They were delayed by this crowd and another spontaneous healing. Before they could reach their destination a servant of Jairus' house found them and told Jairus his daughter had died. Seeing Jairus' grief Jesus turned to him and told him to have faith, all would be well. When they arrived at the home Jesus sent away the crowd, the mourners who had gathered, and most of His disciples. Taking Jairus, his wife, and the apostles Peter, John, and James, Jesus sat next to the lifeless body of Jairus' daughter. Taking her by the hand Jesus commanded her to sit up. Immediately she returned to life and stood up asking for something to eat. The beloved daughter of Jairus was healed, a living testament to the astonishing power of Jesus Christ.

Read the story of Jairus' daughter in Mark 5:21-43 and Luke 8:40-56.

NEW
TESTAMENT
GOSPELS

Jochebed

... she saved her son from death.

Jochebed was a Hebrew woman of the tribe of Levi who lived around 1500BC. She is notable for her trust in the Lord and reliance upon Him to protect her children when she could not.

At the end of Jacob's life there was a great famine, so he took his large family away from the lands of his fathers and settled in Egypt. Generations later this family had thrived and grown into the Hebrew nation. The Pharaoh of the time grew afraid of the Hebrews ever-increasing strength and sought to control them by forcing them into slavery. Though the lives of the Hebrews became bitter, they continued to flourish in number. The Pharaoh, fearful of an uprising, commanded that all Hebrew baby boys be put to death and drowned in the Nile.

In this time of horror and death a Levite woman named Jochebed gave birth to a son. She kept him hidden for three months but as he grew, she could no longer keep him away from the eyes of the Egyptians. In an act of faith Jochebed wove a basket, placed the infant into it, and hid him among the reeds of the river Nile. There the baby was discovered by the Pharaoh's daughter who immediately recognised him as a Hebrew and was filled with compassion for him.

Pharaoh's daughter adopted him and gave him the name Moses. He was still very young and the daughter required a wet nurse for him. Miriam, the older sister of Moses, asked if she would like a Hebrew wet nurse and when she agreed Miriam retrieved Jochebed. Jochebed was then allowed to raise her precious baby Moses until he was weaned. She then returned him to the Pharaoh's daughter. Jochebed's great faithfulness and courage saved her son from death. In turn Moses would deliver her people from their slavery and into the Promised Land.

Read Jochebed's story in Exodus 2:1-10 and Exodus 6:20.

Leah and Rachel

… the devoted mothers of Israel.

Leah and Rachel were sisters from Harran who lived around 1700BC. Their story is one of intense sorrow and jealousy, but is also a testament to their dedication as mothers and their commitment to the Lord.

Jacob, the grandson of Abraham, travelled to the territory of Harran to find a wife. One day he came upon a well and witnessed a young shepherdess watering her flock. Her name was Rachel and she extended a hand of greeting and hospitality towards him. Jacob was enchanted by her beauty and he immediately fell in love with her. Her father Laban agreed to give her hand in marriage to Jacob in exchange for seven years of hard work. Besotted by Rachel, Jacob willingly agreed. Seven years passed and the day of the wedding arrived. However, Laban tricked Jacob by sending Leah, Rachel's older sister, to the marriage bed in place of Rachel. In the morning Jacob discovered the deception and was outraged. Grieved and betrayed Jacob still longed for Rachel and agreed to work a further seven years for Laban in exchange for Rachel as a second bride.

As Jacob's true love Rachel enjoyed a place of privilege, even though she was barren and endured great sorrow and shame. Leah was unwanted by her husband and so she cried out in misery to the Lord. Knowing she would never be loved by Jacob the Lord blessed Leah with six sons and one daughter. Her abundant children set her at odds with Rachel and they spent years resentfully fighting each other. It was not until years later that God remembered Rachel's despair and blessed her with two sons. She died in childbirth praising the Lord. Her sister Leah never earned Jacob's affection however she showed great faithfulness towards God and was a devoted mother.

Read the story of Leah and Rachel in Genesis 29:1-30:21 and Genesis 35:16-20.

OLD
TESTAMENT

LAWS

Lydia

… the Lord opened her heart.

Lydia was a Greek woman living in Philippi around 50AD. She was a generous woman, dedicated to serving the Lord and aiding her fellow Christians.

During the time of the Acts in the city of Thyatira, within the Philippian province, lived a Greek woman by the name of Lydia who was a merchant of purple cloth. She was considered a wealthy business woman who had a large household with servants. She was also a woman of faith who had converted to Judaism and worshipped God wholeheartedly. Regularly she would gather with other Jewish woman to give praise and pray on the Sabbath.

One Sabbath morning the women were gathered near the city gate when two men, Paul and Silas, came and sat with them. Paul and Silas spoke with the women about the person and work of Jesus. As she sat and listened, Lydia's heart was opened to the good news of Jesus and she was moved to accept Christ as her Saviour. So passionate and complete was her conversion that she immediately went home and gathered every member of her family and all her servants, and brought them back to Paul and Silas so they could also hear the Word. Lydia, and her entire household, were baptised that day.

After to her conversion Lydia offered her home as a location for Paul and Silas to continue their ministry from, making her home the first church in Philippi. She continued to be generous with her financial blessings, not only by encouraging and supporting Paul and Silas during their mission to Philippi, but also making sure the church supported them for many years after. Lydia's great passion for the word of the Lord made her an instrumental member of her growing faith community and also a woman who was deeply trusted by Paul.

Read Lydia's story in Acts 16:11-15.

38

… I am the Lord's servant.

Mary was a Jewish woman born in Galilee around 20BC. Her story is one of faith in the face of trials, grace through doubt, and selfless sacrifice.

A young woman named Mary lived with her family in Galilee. She was descended from the line of King David and was betrothed to be married to an upstanding man from her village named Joseph. One day she was visited by the angel Gabriel. The angel informed her that she would bear a son whom she was to name Jesus. He would be the Son of God, the Immanuel, King of Kings, and Light of the World. Though she was afraid, Mary accepted the will of God in her life and conceived through the Holy Spirit.

Throughout her pregnancy few believed Mary and she faced rejection not only from her family but from her betrothed Joseph. It was only through a divinely inspired dream that Joseph was urged to continue his engagement to Mary. Through all these trials Mary's faith never wavered. Later, after being compelled to travel to Bethlehem for a Roman census, Mary gave birth to her son in a stable. She wrapped Him in simple cloth and laid Him in a manger for she had nowhere else to let Him rest. She loved the little Jesus with her whole heart and spent her life raising and caring for the boy who would one day become the Messiah.

Mary went on to become a Christian believer and was present at the death of Jesus and His appearance to the disciples after His resurrection. Mary's life was one full of faith and she was made notable for her grace, her strength, and her willingness to accept each trial God placed before her.

Read Mary's story in Luke 1:26-56 and Luke 2:1-21.

NEW
TESTAMENT

GOSPELS

Mary and Martha

... I believe that You are the Christ, the Son of God.

Mary and Martha were sisters from Judea who lived around 30AD in the town of Bethany. Their story is one of doubt turned to faith and standing firm in their belief in Jesus as the great healer.

Mary and Martha were first introduced in the Gospel of Luke when they, along with their brother Lazarus, invited Jesus and His disciples to stay with them in their home at Bethany. During His stay with the sisters Martha was anxiously making preparations and providing for her many guests. Her sister Mary did not help but instead sat at the feet of Jesus and listened to His teachings. Martha asked Jesus to tell her sister to help but Jesus gently rebuked her saying that Mary had chosen what was better and that Martha should not be upset. Mary, Martha, and Lazarus all committed themselves as disciples to Jesus and He became close to them; forging a deep and lasting friendship.

Later Lazarus became very ill. Concerned for their brother Mary and Martha sent word to Jesus who was nearby in Jerusalem. Upon receiving the news Jesus replied that He would come but remained where He was for two days. By the time Jesus arrived in Bethany it had been four days since Lazarus had died and was buried. When Jesus arrived and greeted the grieving Martha, she asked why He had delayed in coming saying that He could have healed Lazarus. Jesus asked her who she believed Him to be. Martha replied that He is Christ the Lord. Mary also believed that Jesus could have prevented the death. Jesus was deeply moved by their grief and told them to believe for He would show God's glory. Jesus called into the tomb and immediately Lazarus was raised from the dead. Mary and Martha were overjoyed and continued to follow Jesus and His teachings.

Read the story of Mary and Martha in Luke 10:38-42 and John 11:1-44.

Mary Magdalene

... I have seen the Lord.

Mary Magdalene was a Galilean woman who lived around 30AD. Her story is defined by her incredible transformation, faithful dedication to the Lord, and her place of prominence among the early followers of Jesus.

Mary was first introduced in the Gospel of Luke during a time when Jesus was travelling with his disciples preaching and teaching to the Jews. When Jesus arrived in the Galilean town of Magdala, Mary was brought to Him. Possessed by seven demons she was battered and bruised. With a few words Jesus cast out the demons and healed her. Mary was overwhelmed with gratitude and soon believed in Christ as Lord, choosing to become one of Jesus' followers. She joined the other women who travelled with Jesus and provided for His physical and financial needs.

Mary's faith in her Saviour was so deep that years later, when Jesus was arrested at the behest of the Pharisees, she was one of the few brave disciples who stayed by His side. She stood at the foot of the cross and wept in grief as Jesus died. Mary was also among the women who were the first to go to Jesus' tomb to prepare His body for burial three days after His death. Upon finding the tomb to be empty she rushed back to the apostles. Peter and James returned with her and saw the empty tomb. After they left Mary lingered, confused and grief-stricken. There she was the first to see Jesus in glory after His resurrection.

Mary went on to become one of the foundational members of the early church. Her life is a powerful example of the healing work Jesus Christ performed, but also of a woman who loved her Lord and steadfastly supported His ministry.

Read Mary Magdalene's story in Luke 8:1-3 and John 20:1-18.

OLD
TESTAMENT
GOSPELS

Miriam

... she took a timbrel in her hands and sang to the Lord.

Miriam was a Hebrew woman who lived around 1530BC in Egypt as a slave. Her extraordinary faith gave her strength and hope throughout a life marked by suffering and trials.

Within the Hebrew tribe of Levi a man named Amram married a Levite woman named Jochebed. Together they had a family. They had a daughter Miriam and two sons named Aaron and Moses. The Hebrews were greatly oppressed by the Pharaoh of Egypt and Miriam suffered alongside them. However even as a child, she had faith in the Lord to deliver her people and hope that He would send His prophet to them. Resilient and wise as a young girl, Miriam intervened and saved the life of her baby brother Moses. In doing so she also secured the future of her people as Moses would one day lead them out of Egypt.

As an adult Miriam remained close to God and steadfast in her hope of freedom. She became a prophetess and poet always sharing her unshakable faith with her people. After the Hebrews were liberated from slavery to the Egyptians. It was Miriam who took up her timbrel. She led them in singing praises to the Lord for His deliverance along the shores of the Red Sea. Her wisdom made her remarkable and she grew to be a strong spiritual leader alongside her brothers Aaron and Moses. As the Hebrews wandered the wilderness, she was a source of comfort and guidance to the people and her death was grieved by all.

Miriam was not infallible and made some very public mistakes, but in the end, she was known and praised among her people as a faithful and wise leader.

Read the story of Miriam in Exodus 2:1-10, Exodus 15:1-21 and Numbers 12:1-16.

OLD
TESTAMENT

KINGDOM

Naaman's Maid

... the prophet in Samaria would cure him.

Naaman's maid was a young Israelite girl kidnapped in a battle between Aram and Israel around 870BC. Her devotion to her captors, despite their actions, resulted in Naaman being cured of leprosy.

During a military invasion of Israel, Naaman, who was a commander of the King of Aram's army, captured a young Israelite girl. Naaman took the girl to his home where she served his wife as her maid. Despite being stolen from her own family and being among pagan believers, the girl overtime became a devoted servant who remained faithful to the Lord. Some years later Naaman grew ill with leprosy. Distressed by the impact of his illness upon her master and mistress, the young maid approached Naaman. She suggested that he travel to see the prophet Elisha. Naaman trusted the word and faith of the maid and went to Samaria in Israel with extravagant gifts for Elisha. Two weeks passed as Naaman's wife and her maid waited anxiously.

When Naaman returned his leprosy had been cured. Naaman told the household how Elisha's servant had told him to bathe in the dirty water of the Jordan. Pridefully Naaman had initially refused but, at the encouragement of his own servant, he had washed. Healed and cleansed Naaman thanked Elisha and returned to his own household. From that time Naaman's dedicated his household to serving the Lord God. He laid soil collected in Israel upon his alters and brought burnt offerings only to the God of Israel. The faith of the young maid was rewarded as she was finally free to worship the God her parents had lovingly raised her to honour. Despite having no known name, nor speaking more than a few words, Naaman's maid was a powerful witness for God. Her devotion to her captors demonstrated a forgiving heart and led to an outpouring of blessings to those around her.

Read the story of Naaman's maid in 2 Kings 5:1-27.

OLD
TESTAMENT

KINGDOM

Naomi

... the Lord has not stopped showing His kindness.

Naomi was an Israelite woman who was born around 1060BC. Her story is one of transformation through faith, from bitterness to joy.

In the days of the Israelite judges a great famine impacted the whole land. In an effort to provide for his family a man named Elimelech, from the tribe of Benjamin, moved to Moab with his wife Naomi and their two sons Mahlon and Kilion. Elimelech sickened and died leaving Naomi a widow. Tragically both Mahlon and Kilion also died leaving Naomi responsible for her two widowed Moabite daughter-in-laws. Hopeless and with nothing left in Moab Naomi decided to move back to her hometown of Bethlehem. Only one of her daughters-in-law, Ruth, faithfully followed Naomi. In Israel Naomi's heart became bitter. She blamed the Lord for her misfortunes and deeply grieved the loss of her husband and sons.

As Naomi and Ruth worked together to make a new life, Naomi began see to the Lord's hand of renewal. Ruth caught the eye of Boaz who was the kinsman-redeemer of the family. In her heart Naomi knew that the Lord was providing a means of protection for her and Ruth. Naomi was assured that the Lord had repaired her family when Boaz accepted Ruth's unorthodox marriage proposal.

The walls of bitterness which Naomi had built around her heart came down entirely after Ruth married Boaz and gave birth to a son. Ruth and Boaz gave this son, named Obed, to Naomi to call her own. The women of the city rejoiced that Naomi's life had been renewed and sustained in her old age. When Naomi allowed herself to see the loving actions of the Lord her bitterness was turned to joy.

Read Naomi's story in the book of Ruth.

OLD
TESTAMENT

KINGDOM

Phoebe

... she is a humble servant of the Lord.

Phoebe was a Greek woman who lived around 57AD. She is known not by her profession, or by her husband, but by the words Paul spoke of her as a woman worthy of blessing and welcome.

Paul's spiritual calling to plant churches resulted in faith communities being founded in many cities. In Rome churches had already been established by faithful workers and Paul wrote to them with words of encouragement. In his letter Paul informed them that he had sent them a woman named Phoebe of the church in Cenchreae, a seaport town not far from Corinth.

Like many New Testament women who worked so diligently for the church Phoebe is mentioned only once in scripture. Though he used few words Paul described Phoebe as a woman of godly and noble character. He does this by giving her three titles of distinction. First, he spoke of her as his sister in Christ. Only occasionally did Paul bestow familial titles upon fellow believers, most notably upon Timothy who he calls a son in the faith. Second, he distinguished her as a deaconess. Though many New Testament women deserved of the title of deaconess only Phoebe is called one by Paul. Finally, Paul called her a benefactor; a woman of wealth who used her finances to help many in need. These three titles gave a testimony of a woman whose deep faith prompted her to dutifully care for the physical and spiritual needs of the poor in her community. While it is not known how long Phoebe remained with the Roman churches, nor what acts of service she performed during her time there her character and life echo through the ages as a powerful example. It is not the words Paul wrote of her that distinguished Phoebe but her heartfelt and genuine dedication to spreading the gospel and caring for the community of believers.

Read the words spoken of Phoebe in Romans 16:1-2.

NEW
TESTAMENT
CHURCH

Priscilla

... she is my fellow worker in Christ.

Priscilla was Jewish woman living in Rome around 50AD. Her story is one of fearless bravery and willing service to the Lord wherever He sent her.

In the days of the Acts there was a Jewish woman named Priscilla who lived with her husband Aquila in Rome. They were faithful Jews and regularly visited the synagogue to fellowship and pray. Due to ongoing civil unrest all Jews were ordered out of Rome, so Aquila and Priscilla travelled to Corinth. They attended a Corinthian synagogue where they met the apostle Paul. Paul was preaching to the Jews, most of whom fiercely resisted the word. Despite this resistance the saving message of Jesus Christ settled deeply into the heart and soul of Priscilla and she along with Aquila became believers.

After this Paul continued to teach them, live with them, and share in their tent-making profession. Priscilla and Aquila formed the foundation of the church in Corinth and dutifully ministered to the Christians there. Later Paul was attacked by the Jews and he departed for Ephesus. Aquila and Priscilla accompanied him courageously leaving behind their home and beloved faith community. Paul remained in Ephesus for only a short time before he moved on. Priscilla and Aquila remained there and boldly proclaimed the salvation message bringing many people to faith.

Priscilla continued to have a powerful impact in the new church as she and her husband mentored new believers. Most notable of these was a man named Apollos. Under Priscilla and Aquila's guidance he became a mighty evangelist capable of debating even the most zealous religious leaders. A teacher, dedicated wife, and faithful servant of Jesus, Priscilla was an extraordinary leader and a pillar of the churches in the New Testament.

Read the story of Priscilla Acts 18:1-28.

Puah & Shiphrah

... because they feared God He blessed them.

Puah and Shiphrah were Hebrew women who lived around 1300 BC. They were distinguished as women of great courage and a strong desire to protect the vulnerable.

At the end of his life Jacob, his sons, and their families all moved to Egypt to escape a great famine. After the death of Jacob these families remained in Egypt where they grew in number and became known as the Hebrews. As years went by Pharaoh began to fear that the Hebrews would rise against them. So he decreed that they would be enslaved and set masters over them to oppress them. Even as they endured the misery of slavery, the Hebrews continued to increase in number.

Fearful of this, Pharaoh met with Puah and Shiphrah, the two Hebrew midwives that delivered the babies of Hebrew women. Pharaoh ordered them to attend the births according to their customs, but to ensure that no baby boys lived. Puah and Shiphrah feared the Lord God and knew such actions were sinful, so they did not follow the Pharaoh's demand. When it became apparent Hebrew boys were surviving their births, Pharaoh summoned Puah and Shiphrah back into his presence and demanded to know why they had disobeyed him. Cleverly, Puah and Shiphrah insisted that they could not enact his orders because the Hebrew women were so healthy and would give birth before they arrived to assist. Pharaoh believed the midwives, and instead ordered his Egyptian soldiers to kill the Hebrew baby boys by throwing them into the Nile.

Puah and Shiphrah's act of defiance and bravery saved the lives of many babies. God was pleased with their actions. He blessed Puah and Shiphrah for their faithfulness and goodness by giving each of them families and children of their own.

Read Puah and Shiphrah's story in Exodus 1:8-21.

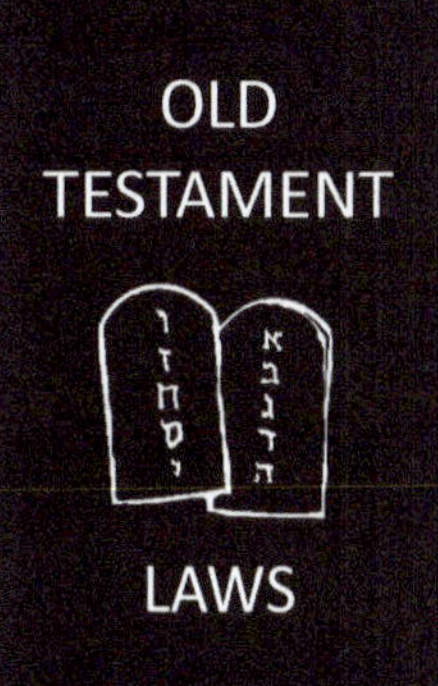
OLD
TESTAMENT

LAWS

Queen of Sheba

...praise be to the Lord your God who has delighted in you.

The Queen of Sheba was an African queen who lived around 940BC. A great and wealthy ruler she sought to know God and to serve Him.

When King Solomon ruled Israel, news of his wealth and wisdom spread through the lands to many nations. The Queen from region near Ethiopia called Sheba could not believe that such wisdom was possible. She decided to visit Solomon and question him. The Queen was wealthy in her own right and she arrived in Jerusalem with a great number of camels carrying spices, large quantities of gold, and precious stones. Such riches had never been seen before even in the wealthy nation of Israel. The Queen presented these gifts to Solomon and then proceeded with her intense investigation, asking every question imaginable.

There was no question Solomon could not answer and the Queen was in awe of his intelligence. She discovered that not only were the reports of Solomon's wisdom understated, the wealth which Solomon had accumulated was beyond imagination. Though her visit had been motivated by incredulous disbelief, the Queen came to see that the nation of Israel had been blessed. Nothing in Israel was done poorly and every individual was cared for. The Queen realised that these blessings could only be from a holy and all-knowing God, who out of great love appointed Solomon as king.

The Queen of Sheba humbled herself and praised the true God of Israel. As she prepared to return to her home Solomon farewelled her by gifting her immense riches. But her true gift was the change in her own heart which was filled with praise for God's eternal love for His people.

Read the Queen of Sheba's story in 1 Kings 10:1-13 and 2 Chronicles 9:1-12.

OLD
TESTAMENT

KINGDOM

Rahab

... may the Lord show kindness to me for I have sheltered you.

Rahab was a Canaanite woman who lived in the city of Jericho around 1400BC. Considered by the Israelites as a gentile she demonstrated great courage and earned a place in the genealogy of Jesus.

After the Israelites failed to trust God's plan to give them the Promised Land, they wandered the wilderness for forty years as divine punishment for their sins and doubt. At the appointed time the Lord told them to re-enter the Promised Land and claim the country God had set aside for them. To do this the Israelites had to clear the land of the gentile nations. The first city in Canaan to be conquered was the great city of Jericho. Encircled by a stone wall the city was well guarded and seemed to be an impenetrable, defiant obstacle.

The Israelites decided to send two spies into the city to determine how strong the people of Jericho were. Upon entering the city, the spies were immediately in grave danger. Prompted by the Lord a prostitute named Rahab offered shelter and protection in her home for the spies. Rahab hid them on her roof under stalks of flax. When city officials and soldiers came to her home to enquire about the spies Rahab sent them in the opposite direction, out of the city. The spies were grateful for her courageous actions. Rahab then helped the spies escape and requested that in return for saving their lives, the Israelites would spare her life and the lives of her family when they attacked Jericho. When the walls of Jericho fell Rahab's house, which was built as part of the wall, remained intact. Rahab and those in her household survived because of her kindness and bravery. Rahab eventually married Salmon, one of the spies she saved, and she became named in the ancestral line of Jesus.

Read Rahab's story in Joshua 2:1-22 and Joshua 6:15-25.

OLD
TESTAMENT

KINGDOM

Rebekah

... because I believe I will go.

Rebekah was a Chaldean woman who lived around 1800BC. Her story is one of the courage it takes to answer God's call and of faithfulness rewarded.

When Abraham was very old he became worried about his son Isaac who was unmarried. Abraham did not want Isaac to marry one of the daughters of the local tribes as they were ungodly, and he was concerned they would lead Isaac astray from the true God. Abraham sent a trusted servant to his homeland to find Isaac a wife. When the servant arrived at Nahor he prayed for God to specifically show him the woman Isaac would marry. Before the servant had even finished his prayers Rebekah arrived to draw water from the well. She offered the servant water and she also offered to give water to all of his camels. When the servant enquired about Rebekah's family lineage, she confirmed she was connected to Abraham's family. At that moment the servant knew this was the woman God had chosen to be Isaac's wife.

The servant was invited by Rebekah's family to rest for the night in their home. Before eating the evening feast the servant relayed Abraham's wishes for Isaac to have a wife, and his answered prayers at the well. Rebekah's family heard the call of God in the servant's story and agreed to the marriage but were reluctant for Rebekah to leave quickly. The family gave Rebekah the choice and with a prayerful heart Rebekah chose to leave with the servant immediately. When the servant and Rebekah arrived at the home of Abraham, Isaac instantly fell in love with her.

Rebekah's faith gave her the immense courage needed to leave her family behind to marry a man she had never met. Her life with Isaac was a happy one and she became the mother to Esau, and to Jacob who would go on to be the Father of all Israel.

Read Rebekah's story in Genesis 24:1-66.

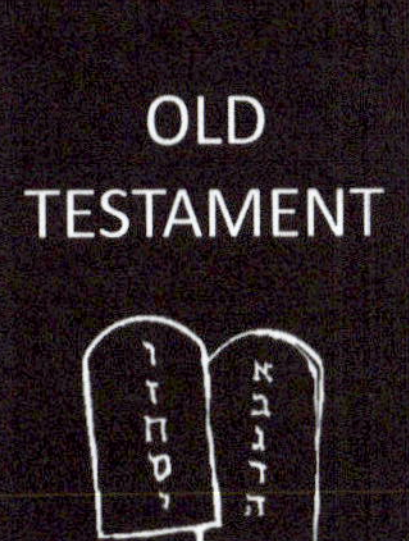
OLD
TESTAMENT

LAWS

Rhoda

... she was overjoyed.

Rhoda was a servant of unknown age and origin who lived in Jerusalem around 44AD. She is known for her enthusiasm and joy.

During the time of the Acts the church in Judea was enduring considerable persecution from King Herod. James, the brother of John, had been put to death. Peter had been arrested and was under constant guard by two soldiers as he waited for his trial. Distressed and uncertain, the believers did they only thing they could. They gathered at the house of Mary, the mother of Mark, and they prayed.

Rhoda, a servant of the family, was praying with all the believers when she heard a knock at the outer door entrance. As she greeted the guest at the door she immediately recognised Peter's voice. Rhoda was so overjoyed she forgot to open the door and instead raced to tell her mistress and the others gathered of the good news. She was met with disbelief and called mad, some people concluded it must have been the ghost of Peter. Rhoda, despite all the doubt, continued to insist that Peter was at the door and that the Lord had answered their prayers.

Meanwhile Peter patiently continued knocking. Eventually the door was opened and Peter was welcomed with astonishment and immense joy. The believers were filled with excitement but Peter called them to be quiet as he told them how the Lord had brought him out of prison. A plan was put in place for Peter to meet with James, the brother of Jesus, and so Peter left. The joy that Rhoda experienced was now the joy which all the believers shared. Rhoda had seen God's power at work and even when others doubted, she never stopped believing in the God who answers the prayers of His people.

Read the story of Rhoda in Acts 12:1-17.

NEW
TESTAMENT
CHURCH

Ruth

... your God will be my God.

Ruth was a Moabite woman who was born around 1040BC. Her story is one of great suffering and grief overcome by a deep faith in the Lord God and her love of her mother-in-law Naomi.

While she was living in Moab, Ruth married an Israelite man named Mahlon, the son of Naomi. Tragically Mahlon, his brother Kilion and their father Elimelech all died within a short time of each other. This left Ruth, Naomi, and Kilion's wife Orpah widowed. Consumed by grief Naomi decided to return home to Bethlehem. Naomi told her Moabite daughter-in-laws to remain with their own families but Ruth refused to so, declaring that Naomi's God was her God and she would always follow Naomi.

Upon their return to Bethlehem Ruth took on the responsibility of providing for Naomi's needs. Her dutiful care was noticed by the whole community. Ruth had left her family, her people, and her land because of her commitment to Naomi and the God of Israel. Seeking to provide food Ruth gleaned barley at the edges of a field, a custom which enabled the poor to survive. Ordinarily such gleaning would render only a small amount of harvest, however Ruth came home with far more barley than could have been expected. Naomi realised that the owner of the field, a man named Boaz, had shown Ruth great compassion and favour. Once Naomi realised Boaz was a near relative and a kinsman redeemer, Naomi instructed Ruth on how to secure a marriage with him.

As a faithful and dutiful daughter, Ruth followed Naomi's every word and soon married Boaz. Their marriage saved Naomi and Ruth from a life of poverty. Ruth's obedience and courage distinguished her as a woman of commitment, grace, and godliness. She eventually became an ancestor of King David and is one of the few women named in Jesus' genealogy.

Read the story of Ruth in the book of Ruth.

Sarah

... God has brought me laughter.

Sarah, previously known as Sarai, was a Chaldean woman who lived around 1830BC. She is known for her alluring beauty and for the joys and struggles she endured.

Before the days of the Israelites, a Chaldean man named Abram was chosen by God to be the father of a blessed nation. God promised that Abram and his wife Sarai would have children of their own, but the promise was not fulfilled immediately. After being barren for eleven years Sarai in an act of disobedience, gave her handmaiden Hagar to Abram in the hope of her conceiving a son. Hagar gave birth to a son but he was not the promised son through which God would create a chosen nation. As the boy grew Sarai realised she was well beyond her childbearing years, and she lost faith that she would ever have a child of her own.

When Abram was 99 years old and Sarai was 89, God held a special circumcision covenant ceremony. At that time God renamed Abram to Abraham, the father of many nations. Sarai was renamed Sarah, the mother of nations. It had now been 25 years since the first promise of a child and even Abraham had given up.

Despite their lost hope three angels visited Abraham a year later and reaffirmed that God would bless him with a child born to him by Sarah. Sarah overheard this conversation and laughed in disbelief. A year later Sarah became pregnant and gave birth to a son, Isaac. When Isaac was eight days old Abraham took him to be circumcised and dedicated him to the Lord God. As he did so Sarah praised the Lord, laughing with joy, and thanking Him for His abundant blessings and faithfulness.

Read Sarah's story in Genesis 16:1-15, Genesis 18:1-15 and Genesis 21:1-7.

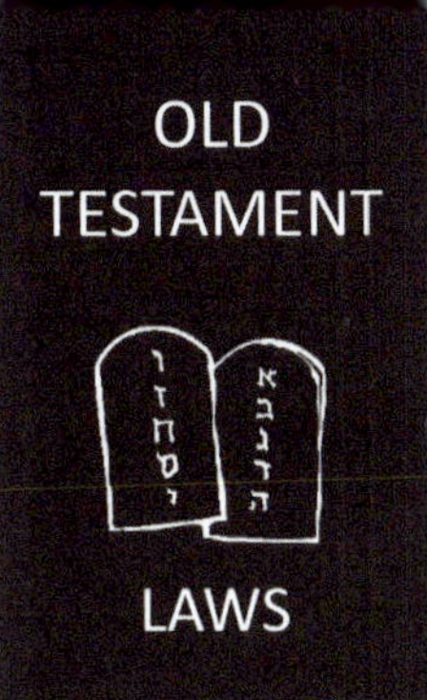

Samaritan Woman

... I know the Messiah is coming.

The Samaritan woman whom Jesus met at the well was born in the town of Sychar around 5BC. Her story is one of transformation through the freedom found by faith in Jesus Christ.

In the early days of His ministry Jesus and His disciples were travelling from Judea to Galilee. Their route took them through Samaria to a town called Sychar where Jacob's Well is located. It was the middle of the day when they arrived so Jesus sent all of the disciples into the town to get food while He waited at the well.

At that time a Samaritan woman came to the well to draw water. Aside from her reputation little is known about this woman, not even her name. She was living with a man who wasn't her husband and she had previously been married five times. The community was ashamed of her choices and rejected her. This is why the Samaritan woman chose to draw water at midday when no one else would be at the well. Jesus looked upon her with compassion and took the time to talk with her about her life. Initially the woman was confused by the analogy Jesus used of living water. But as Jesus patiently talked with her, the woman recognised Jesus as the Messiah and understood her need for salvation.

When the disciples returned the Samaritan woman went back to her town to share the good news she had heard. Despite being treated so terribly by her community, the Samaritan woman knew that her fellow Samaritans needed to meet Jesus. Her selfless testimony resulted in many people in the town confessing that Jesus is Lord. The Samaritan woman showed compassion and mercy by not hoarding the news of the love and peace of Jesus, instead choosing to share this news with joy.

Read the story of the Samaritan Woman in John 4:1-42.

NEW
TESTAMENT

GOSPELS

Tabitha

... she was always doing good deeds before the Lord.

Tabitha was a Greek woman who lived in Joppa, a town in Israel, around 35AD. Her life was marked by dutiful service to the poor in her town.

Tabitha, also known as Dorcas, was a Greek woman living in Joppa, Israel. Tabitha had become a Christian within two years after the death and resurrection of Jesus. She dedicated her life to serving the poor and widowed who lived in her town by providing robes and clothing. It was the community who testified that Tabitha was always doing good.

Tabitha was so beloved by the Christian community that when she suddenly became ill and died, they could not bear to bury her. Instead they washed her body and placed her in an upstairs room. They then sent two emissaries to Peter who was currently ministering in a nearby town called Lydda. The emissaries begged Peter to please come at once. When Peter arrived in the town of Joppa he went to the upstairs room where Tabitha's body had been placed. There he found the room full of widows weeping and mourning for Tabitha. Peter sent them all out of the room and got down on his knees and prayed. As he prayed the Lord resurrected Tabitha to life. She went on to continue to serve among the poor and the widowed.

Throughout the telling of this event Tabitha's words are not recorded. Instead her story is told by the witnesses and community members who declared of her charitable works, and deeply mourned her death. Her life and faith are not just a testimony to the power of Jesus over death, but an example of the richness of a life lived with generosity and compassion.

Read about Tabitha in Acts 9:36-43.

NEW
TESTAMENT
CHURCH

Tamar

... do not harm her for she is righteous.

Tamar was a Canaanite woman who lived around 1670BC. Her story is one ingenuity and determination born from grave injustice.

Judah, one of the twelve sons of Jacob, left the household of his father and married a woman named Shua. Together they had three sons named Er, Onan, and Shelah. When Er came of age Judah obtained a Canaanite wife for him named Tamar. Before long Er had done great evil in the eyes of the Lord and was put to death. In accordance with Hebrew tradition Tamar was given though marriage to Judah's next son, Onan. It was hoped that Tamar would give birth to a son through Onan to inherit Er's properties and wealth. Onan did not want this to happen so he denied Tamar. This was sinful in the eyes of the Lord who also put Onan to death. Judah was so afraid after the loss of two of his sons that he did not allow Tamar to marry his remaining son, Shelah, as was law. Instead, Judah sent Tamar back to her own family to live in shame as a childless widow.

Years later after the death of his wife, Judah travelled past the house of Tamar's father. Unsatisfied with her fate as a forgotten widow, Tamar veiled her face and stood by the road waiting for Judah to pass by. Judah did not recognise Tamar. He believed that she was a temple prostitute and slept with her. After taking his seal and staff in place of payment Tamar left. Three months later it was discovered that she was pregnant. Judah was ashamed of Tamar and initially called for her to be burned. Ever shrewd Tamar provided proof that the child she carried was Judah's by sending him his seal and staff. Judah recognised his own unjust treatment of Tamar, humbled himself, and spared her life. Tamar went on to marry Judah and give birth to twin boys. Clever and tenacious Tamar is one of the few women named the genealogy of Jesus.

Read Tamar's story in Genesis 38:1-30.

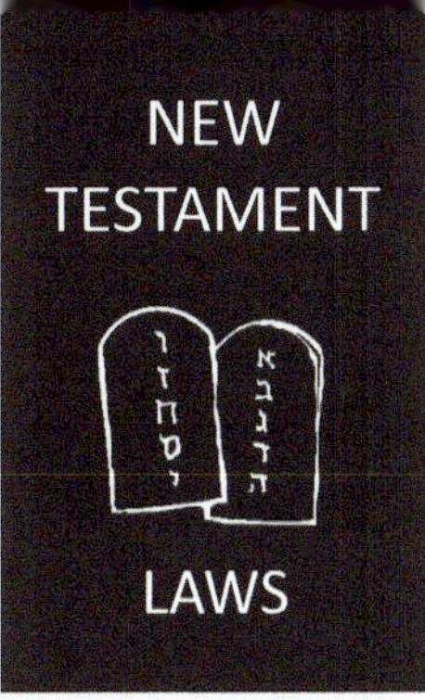

74

Widow of Zaraphath

... the word of the Lord from your mouth is the truth.

The Widow of Zarephath was an unnamed Phoenician woman who lived around 870BC. Her story was one of transformation from utter despair to thanksgiving.

In the days of evil King Ahab the Lord spoke through the prophet Elijah, warning that there would be a great drought. Elijah was a wandering prophet so during the years of drought he was cared for by God in the Kerith Ravine. After Elijah's water source dried up the Lord told Elijah to leave Israel and go to Zarephath, a town in Phoenicia, and that He would provide for Elijah's thirst and hunger there.

When Elijah arrived he found a poor widow gathering sticks to make a fire. She had almost run out of food and was mournfully preparing to cook a final meal for herself and her young son. Elijah approached her and told her not to be afraid. He asked her to make them a small cake from the last of her food. Elijah declared that the Lord would not let the jar of flour run out, or the jug of oil go dry. The widow acted in faith and trusted Elijah. The widow, her son, and Elijah were fed from this alone for the remainder of the drought.

Later the widow faced a greater test of her faith when her only son died of a fever. Overcome by grief and confusion, Elijah prayed. The Lord heard Elijah's cries of despair and the son was raised to life. Even though she was not an Israelite, the widow experienced firsthand the mercies and miracles of the Lord. Through these extraordinary events she came to confess that the Word of the Lord was true. The widow's willingness to make a personal sacrifice ultimately lead to her salvation.

Read the Widow of Zarephath's story in 1 Kings 17:7-24.

NEW
TESTAMENT

KINGDOM

Widow Who Gave All

... in faith she has given her all, more than all the rest.

Little is known about the Widow Who Gave All except that she is a poor, widowed, Jewish woman who lived during the time of Jesus. The faith and sacrifice of the widow were so mighty that she drew the attention and blessing of Jesus.

When Jesus was travelling through Judea, He stopped to teach at the Jewish temple. As Jesus was sitting by the crowd He witnessed the rich putting their money in one of the thirteen trumpet chests that were placed at the temple. While everyone could not help but see and hear the large amount of heavy coins being donated by the rich, a poor widow placed her coin offering into the chest. She went unnoticed and unheard as her offering was too small to draw the attention of anyone, except for Jesus.

The widow's offering was two small coins called "lepta". They were worth 1/64th of a day's wage, barely enough to buy a piece of wood or a small bit of incense. In monetary value it was an insignificant amount. Yet it was this offering that drew the attention of Jesus. He declared to his disciples that the offering of the widow exceeded the largest donation because she had given all she owned without reservation.

The widow was praised by Jesus as a vivid example of what it means to love God "with all your heart, and with all your soul, and with all your mind, and with all your strength." Her selfless act showed the importance of giving everything to God and trusting in the knowledge that it is He who provides. The widow found her purpose in humble generosity and in doing so drew the respect and admiration of Jesus.

Read the story of the Widow Who Gave All in Mark 12:41-44.

NEW
TESTAMENT
GOSPELS

Woman Who Anointed Jesus

...your faith has saved you go in peace.

The Woman Who Anointed Jesus lived around 30 AD. Unnamed and mysterious she is remembered as a redeemed woman who was so moved by Jesus love for her that she adorned Him with her own tears.

During His ministry Jesus was invited to eat at the home of Simon, the Pharisee. Normally the host would provide guests with a bowl of water to wash their feet and greet their guests with a welcoming kiss. Often hosts would pour scented oil onto the head of a guest. When Jesus arrived at Simon's house, Simon deliberately insulted and rejected Jesus by not offering any of these customary welcome rites. As a result Jesus reclined at Simon's table with unwashed, dirty feet and a heavy body odour.

As the dinner progressed an uninvited guest slipped into the house of Simon. Described as the "woman who was a sinner" all the guests viewed her as unwelcome, except for Jesus. Instead Jesus saw her as forgiven, righteous, and welcomed in His presence. Overwhelmed with gratitude for the way Jesus saw and loved her, the woman had come to the house with an alabaster jar of perfume. While Jesus was reclining at the table, the woman knelt at His feet and wept. With her tears she cleansed His feet of all dirt and dust. She took her own hair and dried His feet, then poured perfumed oil upon them.

When Simon began to cast judgement upon the woman and Jesus' response in his thoughts, Jesus rebuked him by telling a pointed parable about the nature of gratitude. Everyone at that meal saw a sinner and condemned her for her past. Jesus saw a woman seeking repentance. Jesus confirmed her spiritual transformation by forgiving her sin, reminding her of her saving faith, and sending her on her way with a blessing of peace.

Read about the Woman Who Anointed Jesus in Luke 7:36-50.

NEW
TESTAMENT
GOSPELS

Zelophehad's Daughters

...the daughters of Zelophehad are right.

Around 1400BC, Zelophehad's daughters united to challenge the laws of the Israelites. Their determined strength caused a change that would allow their family name to continue for generations to come.

After leaving Egypt the people of Israel had been wandering in the wilderness for 40 years as punishment. They believed their spies who said that the inhabitants of the land God had promised them were too strong to be defeated. A census was taken to confirm that a new generation had risen and all the unfaithful had perished. A faithful man of the old generation named Zelophehad had also died. He left behind five daughters, whose names were Mahlah, Noah, Hoglah, Milcah, and Tirzah. Since he had no sons, the descendants of Zelophehad were not able to be counted in the census and because of this, the daughters were not eligible to be given an inheritance of land.

It was expected that Zelophehad's daughters would quietly accept this decree. Instead they came forward and challenged the destiny being imposed on them by Moses, Eleazar the priest, the chieftains, and the whole assembly. The five daughters reminded them of the faithfulness of their father, who had not participated in any sin that should cause his family to be denied an inheritance. His only transgression was not having a son. The daughters of Zelophehad knew that God's law is just. They presented their case with confidence knowing that the current law did not take into account the unusual circumstance of a man without sons. When Moses brought this case before the Lord, it was confirmed that the daughters were right. God Himself responded by changing the law of inheritance from this point on. Zelophehad's daughters offer a compelling lesson of hope for all those faced with seemingly unmovable obstacles.

Read about Zelophehad's daughters in Numbers 26:33, Numbers 27:1-11 and Numbers 36:1-12.

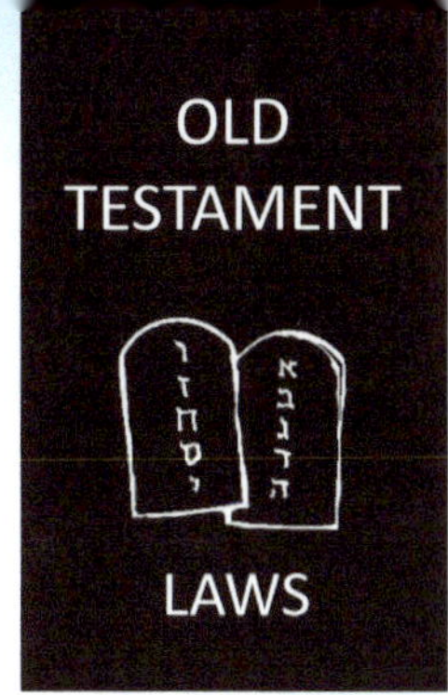

82

Zipporah

...praise be to the Lord who rescued you.

Zipporah was a Midianite woman who was born around 1520BC. She was known for her fearlessness, strength, and loyalty.

During the story of Exodus, Moses killed an Egyptian who had abused a Hebrew slave. Moses fled from Egypt to Midian, home to distant relatives of the Hebrews. One day he was sitting by a well when the seven daughters of Jethro, a Midianite shepherd and priest, came to water their flocks. The daughters were being harassed by competing herdsmen who tried to drive them away. Moses intervened and protected them. He then watered their sheep. The daughters returned to their father Jethro, who welcomed Moses into his tents. Grateful for the actions of Moses, Jethro gave his eldest daughter Zipporah to Moses in marriage.

During their marriage Zipporah gave birth to two sons. Zipporah followed the god of her people and in accordance with their traditions the sons were not circumcised. However, Zipporah demonstrated her faith in the God of Moses in an odd incident. When Moses received God's word through the burning bush, he decided to return to Egypt. The Bible tells that along the way God met Moses and was about to kill him. Sensing the displeasure of the Lord, Zipporah took a knife and circumcised her sons. God was pleased with this and spared the life of Moses.

Soon after Moses returned to Egypt and led the Hebrews out of slavery and through the wilderness. Zipporah proved herself to be a faithful and discerning woman who understood the sovereignty of God, and who bravely followed her husband wherever he wandered.

Read Zipporah's story in Exodus 2:11-22 and Exodus 4:20-26.

NEW
TESTAMENT
LAWS

Models

IN ORDER OF APPEARANCE

Rehema Bwisengo, Anne Mukoma, Gerada Rickard, Georgie Pilgrim, Anne Clarke, Lisa Caulfield, Sarah Tshamala, Corianna Quak, Lynette Delport, Eloise Osborne, Yvonne Bwisengo, Naomi Tshamala, Angele Tshamala, Lorinda James, Corri-Anna Bwisengo, Amelia Rees, Bawili Joel, Tabisangwa Sango, Carmen Brauer, Haneen Sabbagh, Kylie Hanford, Lorraine Guy, Nazreen Curtis, Abigail Tshamala, Helen Cook, Therese Tshiama, Susan Ballard, Bintu Conteh, Teresa Arop, Belesia Masoka, Kierstin Ham, Pia Sunil, Elisha Sunil, Maddie Hanford, Ruth Wilson, Shelley Patuaka, Julie Wilson, Alice Cook, Jess Meek, Lucy Guy, Mayah Guy, Amber Grant, Lydia James & Shelia Jakech.

Background Images

SOURCED FROM UNSPLASH.COM

Images taken by Ales Krivec, Alexandra Dech, Andrei Mike, Antoine Beuvillain, Brian Erickson, Claudio Testa, Claudel Rheault, Daniil Silantev, Delaney Turner, Eddie Stigson, Holly Mandarich, James Lee, Jasper Boer, Jay Nair, Jeff King, Jesse Gardner, Jill Dimond, Johann Siemens, John Purakal, Joseph Barrientos, Jo Vangringerbeek, Julian Schiemann, Katerina Sysolyatina, Kenneth Thewissen, Luca Micheli, Luke Porter, Mojtaba Hoseini, Neonbrand, Oskars Sylwan, Paul Morris, Peter Kent, Quag Jaka, Ramiz Dedakovic, Ryan De Hamer, Sara Deis, Tiago Gerken and Vlad Marisescu.

The photos in this study reflect the diverse community of Christians, from many different cultural and geographic backgrounds, who were connected to Northside Evangelical Church (NEC). The ministry of NEC focused on the local community to help them see, through us, how life changing a relationship with Jesus can be. The ongoing prayer of all those who contributed to the publication of this Women of the Bible book is that many people from diverse cultural and geographic backgrounds would grow in their life changing relationship with Jesus.

Thank you for your support!

Profits from the purchase of this book will be used to support women's charities and organisations close to our hearts.

Notes